Cardiff Libraries
www.cardiff...
D0810045

CARDIFF
FRDYDD

A myth from Ancient Greece

Mal Peet and
Elspeth Graham

Illustrated by
Daria Petrilli

CONTENTS

ACC. No: 03180962

Dear Reader,

How Winter Came into the World is our retelling of an Ancient Greek myth. Myths are stories made up to explain why the world is like it is, or why things happen the way they do. The story of Persephone and Hades tells us why the seasons change.

We don't know whether the Ancient Greeks really believed these explanations. It's just as likely that they simply enjoyed the stories. That's probably why myths like this one have lasted such a long time.

Mal Peet and Elspeth Graham

Chapter 1

Hades, ruler of the Underworld

Deep, deep below the surface of the earth was another world. This world was the colour of gloom. Its forests and flowers were as grey as ash. Its icy rivers flowed without making a sound. Fires burned, but their flames were grey and cold.

This was a world without colour. This was a world without life. This was the Underworld, the home of the ghosts of the dead.

The ruler of the Underworld was Hades, god of the dead. Hades was tall and handsome. His long hair was silver. His eyes were dark and also very sad.

Sad-eyed Hades walked through his kingdom, followed by his ghost-servants. They didn't have much to say. Sometimes, bored out of his mind, Hades would say 'Come on, someone – speak! Tell me a story!'

But dead men tell no tales. The ghosts just moaned, like a winter wind.

Hades was a lonely god.

Hades could not live in the Overworld. He had visited it, just a few times, but the bright light hurt his head. It went into his eyes like splinters, like broken glass. But he had seen the colours up there and he could not forget them. He often thought about them, remembering how rich and beautiful they were, how they changed in sunlight and in shadow. The memory made his eyes tingle with tears.

Hades sat on his throne among his throng of ghosts and sighed. He would have to go up there, up to the Overworld again. It would make his head hurt. It would make his heart ache. But it would be worth it.

Chapter 2

A visit to the Overworld

Hades travelled upwards through secret twisting tunnels and dim caverns. He travelled along tracks and paths deep in grey dust. Up and up and up.

At last, he came to a cave that opened into sunlight. He stumbled through the sunbeams, screwing up his painful eyes. He stood at the entrance to the cave and peered out at the Overworld.

The colours!
How wonderful they were!
He leaned against the rock wall, feeling dizzy
and thrilled.

Hades was looking out at a warm spring
morning. He was looking at a meadow
speckled with wild flowers, white, yellow
and pink. Pale trees stood in their own,
darker shadows.

He remembered the word green. Yes, that was it, 'green'. There were so many different kinds of green in the Overworld. Every plant and tree had its own shade of green, with a darker echo in its shadow on the grass. Hundreds of shades of green! Amazing!

Further away, light danced on a blue sea. Further away still, pale purple mountains rose towards a clear blue sky. Hades grew giddy looking at them.

There were sounds, too. Leaves whispered in the breeze. Animals called in the distance. The sky was full of birdsong.

Hades shaded his eyes with his hand. The brightness of the Overworld was filling his head with pain. He felt that if he gazed at it for just one more minute he would go blind. It was time for him to return, to go back down to the dim grey world that did not hurt his eyes.

At that moment, he heard a voice. The voice of someone alive, someone singing. He turned to see where it was coming from. Then he fell in love. Just like that.

Chapter 3
Persephone

Hades fell in love with a young woman called Persephone. Persephone had skin the colour of honey and hair like black silk. She was walking across the meadow, picking flowers. Her dress was the same blue as the blue of the sky, and she was singing. She was happy and she was very beautiful.

As soon as he saw her, Hades knew that he could not live without her. He didn't stop to think. He just stepped out into the painful sunlight and grabbed Persephone.

He scooped her up and carried her into the cave. He carried her back down the secret paths and twisting tunnels, down towards his Underworld.

Persephone kicked and struggled. Hades felt the warmth of her skin. He had never felt warm skin before. He liked it.

Now, this is a story about gods and goddesses. There aren't any ordinary human people in this story. Persephone was beautiful and warm and scared and angry, but she was not an ordinary human. She was the daughter of gods.

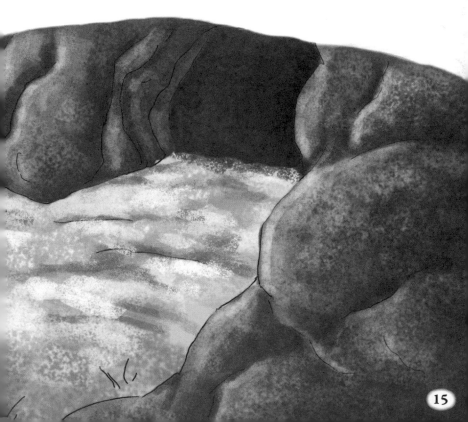

Her father was Zeus, the greatest of the gods. Her mother was Demeter. Demeter was the goddess of all nature, the goddess of all that grows on earth. She made seeds turn into plants. She made buds turn into flowers. She made fruit ripen on trees.

Demeter was a kind and gentle goddess. But when she learned that her daughter Persephone had disappeared she was filled with anger and sadness.

Demeter stopped spreading warmth through the world and it grew cold.

Leaves fell from the trees.

Fruits withered.

The flowers died.

Colour started to fade from the world.

Demeter didn't care. The only thing she cared about was finding Persephone. She raged around the world like a winter wind, searching.

Chapter 4

Zeus has a problem

It was Helios, the sun god, who told
Demeter what had happened. Helios drove
his golden chariot across the sky each day,
watching the earth below him. His bright
eyes saw everything. He had seen Hades steal
Persephone down to the Underworld.

• *Helios:* (say) 'hee-li-uss'.

When Demeter found out what had happened, her anger was terrible. She flew like a storm-cloud to Mount Olympus, the home of the gods, the home of Zeus.

'Hades has stolen our daughter, Persephone,' she screamed.

All Olympus shook. Zeus shook.

'Tell Hades to bring her back!' screamed Demeter. 'Tell him to bring her back NOW! If he does not return Persephone to me nothing will grow in the Overworld again, **EVER.**'

Zeus sat in his throne and stroked his beard, thinking. He had a problem. The problem was this: Hades was his brother, and Zeus loved him.

Hades had always been very sad and very lonely in his Underworld kingdom. Zeus knew this. He understood that Hades needed a queen to rule alongside him. He needed a queen who would bring a little warmth and brightness into his life. Zeus did not want to make his brother unhappy.

But Zeus knew that if Hades did not give Persephone back to Demeter, Demeter would never tend the world again. The seasons would end. Nothing would grow or flower. The Overworld would be as cold and grey as the Underworld.

Zeus called his messenger, Hermes. Hermes had silver skin like a fish, and wings stronger than a swan's.

'Hermes,' said Zeus, 'we have a problem. I want you to go to the Underworld. Tell my brother Hades that he must let Persephone go. Tell him that Demeter will never warm the world again until Persephone is free. Beg my brother to bring her back to her mother.'

Chapter 5

Hermes delivers
a message

Hermes was faster than lightning. He was in
the Underworld in a flash.

Persephone was sitting on a throne of
grey marble. She glowed like a jewel in the
dim, grey light. The sad ghosts gazed at her,
remembering what it was like to be full of life.

Hades sat on his throne next to her. He
was holding her hand. His sad eyes were full
of love.

Near Persephone there was a grey dish of grey fruit, fruit that looked likes stones: grey apples, grey pears, grey grapes. When Hermes saw it, he was worried. He was very worried indeed.

'Persephone, have you eaten any of that?' asked Hermes.

He knew that if she had eaten the food of the Underworld she could not go free. It was the law of the gods that no one who ate the food of the dead could go back to the world of the living. If she had eaten just one grape she was doomed to stay in the Underworld for ever.

Persephone shook her head. She had not eaten the grey fruit. She was very, very hungry, but she couldn't eat grey fruit that looked like stones. Could you?

Hermes delivered his message. He told Hades that Zeus wanted Persephone to return to the Overworld and her mother. He told Hades about Demeter's anger and sadness. He told Hades that the Overworld was growing cold and losing its colour.

Hades listened. He lowered his head, thinking. He could not bear to lose Persephone. But if he kept her, he would never see the beauty of the Overworld again. He would never again see 'green'.

He would never again see light dancing on blue water.

He would never again see flowers opening or hear birdsong. He felt as if his heart was being torn in half.

Persephone was filled with joy at the thought of returning to the world of warmth and colour. But she could also see the hurt in Hades' sad eyes.

'Lord Hades,' she said, softly. 'I could love you. But I could not live forever in your grey world of ghosts. Please take me back to my mother. Please take me back into the light.'

Hades lifted his head. He managed to smile at her.

'I have no choice,' he said.

Chapter 6

The pomegranate seeds

So once again Hades travelled up towards the Overworld, this time with Persephone close behind him.

Up along twisting grey paths they went, through gloomy caverns. Up and up they went, across cold and silent rivers and through silent forests of ash-grey trees.

Near the end
of their journey,
they passed a small
pomegranate tree. Persephone,
without knowing why she
did it, picked a fat grey fruit.
Perhaps she wanted a keepsake,
a souvenir, of her time amongst
the dead. Hades did not see her
do it. His eyes were fixed on the
path ahead.

Now the first pale beams of sunlight reached them. A splash of light fell onto the pomegranate in Persephone's hand. The skin of the grey fruit began to change colour. As more warm sunlight touched it, the pomegranate ripened. It turned a rich yellow, splashed with orange, and speckled with red.

Persephone split the pomegranate open.
Inside, each ripe seed was wrapped in sweet
red flesh. Her mouth watered.

At the mouth of the cave, Hades shaded his eyes with his hand. Then he stepped into the sunlight to where Demeter and Zeus stood waiting. Hades held out his arms to greet his brother. Zeus embraced him, smiling.

At that moment a terrible cry split the air.
It came from Demeter.
Hades whirled around. He saw the
pomegranate in Persephone's hand, grabbed
it, and hurled it back into the darkness of
the cave.

But it was too late. Persephone had eaten three – just three – of the ruby-red seeds. She had eaten the food of the dead. She belonged to the dead. The light of the Overworld stabbed her eyes and she staggered back into the gloom.

Chapter 7
Winter and summer

Demeter's sorrow was terrible. She drew clouds like black curtains across the sky. She sent biting winds to rip the leaves from the trees. She flung ice and bitter rain at the hills. Plants withered. Animals hid. Humans huddled in their homes.

Once again, the gods met on Olympus.

'The world is dying,' Zeus said. 'How can we save it?'

The gods could not agree on an answer. For two days and two nights their huge voices were like thunder rolling down the mountain.

At last Zeus stood up and stamped his mighty foot. The world shook.

'I have decided,' he said. 'Each year Persephone will live in the Underworld for three months. One month for each of the seeds she ate. For the rest of the year she will live in the Overworld with her mother!'

So, for three months each year, Hades was happy. With Persephone beside him, the sadness left his eyes. Her beauty brought a little warmth and colour into his cold grey kingdom.

They sat side by side and she told him stories of the Overworld. She told him about its beauty and its warmth. She described to him the smells of flowers and of the pine woods and of freshly baked bread.

She also taught him the names of all the colours that she could think of, and of others that she could only imagine.

There was love in the Land of the Dead. Even the ghosts cheered up a bit.

But for those same three months Demeter was sick with sadness. For those three months she stopped caring for the world, and the world grew cold. The leaves fell from the trees and the fields were bare. The blue sea turned grey and angry. The flowers shrank back into the ground. Winter came into the world.

Those three months were long and hard for Demeter, and for the Overworld, too. But every year, the winter months passed.

They ended when Persephone returned to Demeter and Demeter's joy lit up the world. The sparkle returned to the sea and soft new leaves appeared on the trees.

Life returned to the fields and forests. Animals who had hidden, sleeping, through the cold time of Demeter's sorrow woke up. They came out into the sunlight, blinking. They saw that the world was filled with colour again. They saw a hundred shades of green. Summer had returned.